TROMBONE GEMS

By H.A. VANDERCOOK

A COLLECTION OF TROMBONE SOLOS WITH PIANO ACCOMPANIMENT

CONTENTS

RUBANK®

HAL•LEONARD®
CORPORATION

7777 W. BLUEMOUND RD. P.O. BOX 13819 MILWAUKEE, WI 53213

Visit Hal Leonard Online at
www.halleonard.com

Written by H.A. Vandercook, *Trombone Gems* has taken some of Rubank's most renowned trombone solos and combined them into a single book/CD collection. This new edition provides a unique approach to the music; tracks 1-10 of the CD provide a full performance for trombone and piano, and tracks 11-20 has piano accompaniment only. After years of remaining the favorite trombone repertoire pieces of students and teachers alike, *Trombone Gems* will be a classically enjoyable and practical addition to any trombone music collection.

By H.A. VANDERCOOK

A COLLECTION OF TROMBONE SOLOS WITH PIANO ACCOMPANIMENT

CONTENTS

7777 W. BLUEMOUND RD. P.O. BOX 13819 MILWAUKEE, WI 53213

Visit Hal Leonard Online at
www.halleonard.com

Written by H.A. Vandercook, *Trombone Gems* has taken some of Rubank's most renowned trombone solos and combined them into a single book/CD collection. This new edition provides a unique approach to the music; tracks 1-10 of the CD provide a full performance for trombone and piano, and tracks 11-20 has piano accompaniment only. After years of remaining the favorite trombone repertoire pieces of students and teachers alike, *Trombone Gems* will be a classically enjoyable and practical addition to any trombone music collection.

RUBY

Moderato

boldly

rit.   *f*   *a tempo*

Ruby

8

Ruby

EMERALD

Copyright MCMXXXVIII by Rubank Inc., Chicago, Ill.
International Copyright Secured

Moderato

TRIO

Emerald

TURQUOISE

Cópyright MCMXXXVIII by Rubank Inc., Chicago, Ill.
International Copyright Secured

14

Moderato

Turquoise

Turquoise

Turquoise

GARNET

Copyright MCMXXXVIII by Rubank Inc., Chicago, Ill.
International Copyright Secured

Moderato

Garnet

Garnet

Garnet

TOPAZ

Moderato

Topaz

Topaz

OPAL

Copyright MCMXXXVIII by Rubank, Inc., Chicago, Ill.
International Copyright Secured

AMETHYST

Andante

Copyright MCMXXXVIII by Rubank, Inc., Chicago, Ill.
International Copyright Secured

Moderato

SAPPHIRE

34

DIAMOND

Copyright MCMXXXVIII by Rubank, Inc., Chicago, Ill.
International Copyright Secured

Moderato

Diamond

Diamond

PEARL

Andante

Copyright MCMXXXVIII by Rubank, Inc., Chicago, Ill.
International Copyright Secured

Moderato

RUBY

EMERALD

Copyright MCMXXXVIII by Rubank Inc., Chicago, Ill.
International Copyright Secured

TURQUOISE

Copyright MCMXXXVIII by Rubank Inc., Chicago, Ill.
International Copyright Secured

GARNET

Copyright MCMXXXVIII by Rubank Inc., Chicago, Ill.
International Copyright Secured

TOPAZ

Copyright MCMXXXVIII by Rubank Inc., Chicago, Ill.
International Copyright Secured

OPAL

Copyright MCMXXXVIII by Rubank, Inc., Chicago, Ill.
International Copyright Secured

AMETHYST

Copyright MCMXXXVIII by Rubank, Inc., Chicago, Ill.
International Copyright Secured

SAPPHIRE

Copyright MCMXXXVIII by Rubank, Inc., Chicago, Ill.
International Copyright Secured

DIAMOND

PEARL

Copyright MCMXXXVIII by Rubank, Inc., Chicago, Ill.
International Copyright Secured